"There's no sort of use in knocking," said the footman

A. E. Jackson

Alice
ILLUSTRATED

120 Images from the Classic Tales of Lewis Carroll

Selected and Edited by
Jeff A. Menges

With an Introduction by
Mark Burstein

Dover Publications, Inc.
Mineola, New York

Bibliographical Note

Alice Illustrated: 120 Images from the Classic Tales of Lewis Carroll, first published by Dover Publications, Inc., in 2012, is an original compilation of images from the following sources: John Tenniel, *Alice's Adventures in Wonderland* (Macmillan and Co., London, 1865) and *Through the Looking Glass and What Alice Found There* (Macmillan and Co., London, 1872); Peter Newel, *Alice's Adventures in Wonderland* (Harper & Brothers, New York, 1901); Arthur Rackham, *Alice's Adventures in Wonderland* (William Heinemann, London, 1907); Charles Robinson, *Alice's Adventures in Wonderland* (Cassell & Co., Ltd., London, 1907); Millicent Sowerby, *Alice in Wonderland* (Chatto & Windus, London, 1907); W. H. Walker, *Alice's Adventures in Wonderland* (John Lane, The Bodley Head, Ltd., London, 1907); Harry Rountree, *Alice's Adventures in Wonderland* (Collins' Clear Type Press, London, 1908); Mabel Lucie Attwell, *Alice in Wonderland* (Raphael Tuck & Sons, Ltd., London, 1910); George Soper, *Alice's Adventures in Wonderland* (George Allen & Unwin, Ltd., London, 1910); A. E. Jackson, *Alice's Adventures in Wonderland* (Henry Frowde: Hodder & Stoughton, London, 1914); Margaret Tarrant, *Alice in Wonderland* (Ward, Lock & Co., Limited, London and Melbourne, 1916); Milo Winter, *Alice's Adventures in Wonderland and Through the Looking Glass* (Rand McNally & Company, Chicago and New York, 1916); Charles Folkard, *Songs from Alice in Wonderland and Through the Looking-Glass* (A. & C. Black, Ltd., London, 1921); Gwynedd Hudson, *Alice's Adventures in Wonderland* (Hodder & Stoughton, Ltd., London, 1922); Willy Pogány, *Alice's Adventures in Wonderland* (E. P. Dutton & Company, New York, 1929); Barry Moser, *Through the Looking-Glass* (University of California Press, Berkeley, Los Angeles, London, 1983). An Introduction has been written by Mark Burstein specially for this edition.

Library of Congress Cataloging-in-Publication Data

Alice illustrated : 120 images from the classic tales of Lewis Carroll / selected and edited by Jeff A. Menges ; with an introduction by Mark Burstein.
    p. cm.
ISBN 978-0-486-48204-0 (pbk.)
ISBN 0-486-48204-9
  1. Carroll, Lewis, 1832–1898. Through the looking-glass—Illustrations. 2. Carroll, Lewis, 1832–1898. Alice's adventures in Wonderland—Illustrations. I. Menges, Jeff A., editor of compilation. II. Burstein, Mark, 1950– writer of added commentary.

PR4611.A73A45 2012
741.6'4—dc23

2011047022

Manufactured in the United States by Courier Corporation
48204901
www.doverpublications.com

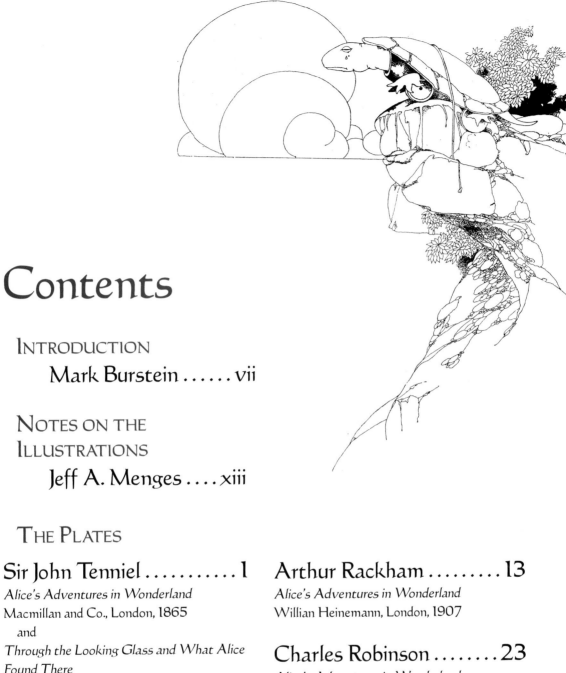

Contents

FRONT MATTER ILLUSTRATIONS

Title page: Harry Rountree
Contents: Charles Robinson
Introduction: Margaret Tarrant
Page ix: Arthur Rackham
Page x: Charles Robinson
The Plates: Millicent Sowerby

Tailpiece: Barry Moser

Introduction

It is one of literature's greatest paradoxes that a book whose author and original illustrator complemented each other with such divine perfection, and whose inextricably intertwined words and images are among the most revered and iconic of Western civilization, has since become the most widely illustrated novel in existence. Several factors are involved: the work's lack of textual descriptions, which engenders a wide artistic license; how deeply and radically it delves into the human psyche, granting artists permission to explore their own versions of the exotic, paradoxical spaces inside Alice's dream worlds; its ubiquity in our culture, calling forth an identification with its heroine or other characters and sparking childhood memories; and, it must be admitted, commercial reasons. These factors will be discussed in depth later. But let us begin—as the King of Hearts instructs us—at the beginning.

The exterior life of the Rev. Charles Lutwidge Dodgson was so monumentally dull that it can satisfactorily be given in its entirely in a few phrases: he was born in 1832 and matriculated at Christ Church, Oxford, in 1851, where he remained as a bachelor and mathematical lecturer until his death in 1898, traveling only once outside of England (to Russia) in 1867. And yet, Dodgson's interior life, usually revealed under the nom de plume Lewis Carroll, was of such a magnitude and magnificence that today, nearly 150 years after a certain boat trip up the Isis (Thames) during which he told an amusing, nonsensical tale to the Dean's three daughters (one of them named Alice), fuels a vast industry of books, movies and television productions, theater, music, merchandise, scholarship, discussion, and websites.

Shortly after the now-famous boat ride on July 4, 1862, Alice Pleasance Liddell, the ten-year-old daughter of Dean Henry George Liddell, asked her friend Mr. Dodgson to write down for her the tale he spontaneously had spun. His handwritten and self-illustrated manuscript, which he called *Alice's Adventures under Ground*, was presented to her in November 1864. He was encouraged by many to expand the volume for publication and did so, nearly doubling its length and adding many scenes and characters, including the Cheshire Cat, the March Hare, the mad Hatter, and the Duchess.

Realizing that his own illustrations, charming as they were (he later published them in a facsimile edition with Macmillan in 1886), would not be well received by a public that had high standards in draughtsmanship, Dodgson sought out John Tenniel, the premier cartoonist for the humorous weekly magazine *Punch,* for the job. Tenniel agreed in April 1864, and the collaboration, while occasionally stormy, resulted in the indelible images we know today.

The work's publication in 1865 (by Macmillan in England) and 1866 (Appleton, in the United States) was immediately—and irrevocably—an unprecedented success with critics and the public, both children and adults, including HRH Queen Victoria herself. This did not go unnoticed by other publishers. Thomas Crowell brought out a fine American edition in 1893 with one color frontispiece, and others, such as M. A. Donohue in 1901, put out unauthorized editions with the Tenniel illustrations. But the proverbial dam burst in 1907, when the British copyright expired.

The Edwardian era in the United Kingdom was a Golden Age for illustrated children's books, including classics such as *The Tale of Peter Rabbit* (1902), *Peter and Wendy* (1911), and, in America, *The Wonderful Wizard of Oz* (1900). The combination of artistic excellence and commercial prowess, unsurprisingly, gave rise to some of the finest illustrated versions of Wonderland we are ever likely to see, in a variety of approaches ranging from the Art Nouveau stylings of Charles Robinson to the fanciful illuminations of Arthur Rackham. Although the volume you hold in your hands highlights the magnificent illustrators of the Golden Age of the Victorian and, particularly, the Edwardian eras, it also includes those of Barry Moser, whose Pennyroyal Alice came out in a fine press edition in 1983, as representative of all that has come after that initial

outpouring. Indeed, in the post-Tenniel years, *Alice's Adventures in Wonderland* (and its 1872 successor, *Through the Looking-Glass*) have attracted literally hundreds of the finest illustrators from all over the world. Among the most famous are Harry Furniss, Beatrix Potter (yet unpublished), Willy Pogány, Marie Laurencin, Max Ernst, Mervyn Peake, Salvador Dalí, Peter Blake, Ralph Steadman, and Helen Oxenbury, and there are scores of lesser-known lights. Add to these the countless illustrators of non-English editions whose names will not be familiar to us: some, of course, are Tenniel knock-offs, but many, particularly the Russians and Eastern Europeans, possess unique and sometimes disturbing visions, coupled with sensational renderings. In addition, there exist the visual concepts of theatrical productions, musicals, and operas, and of filmmakers from Thomas Edison in 1910 through Tim Burton a century later—not to mention comic and manga artists, or the thousands of artists who have not published their work in book form, whose work speaks through original drawings, paintings, prints, T-shirts and other merchandise, and online digital renderings. Every art movement of the last and present centuries has been embraced: Art Nouveau, Art Deco, Surrealism, Pop Art, Photorealism, Minimalism, and fantasy, to name a few.

But now we must further address the question: what makes these particular books so irresistible to artists?

First, the book itself carries few descriptions of the setting or the physical appearance of the characters; Carroll's collaboration with Tenniel—one might more accurately call it art direction—was both a substitute and an enhancement. In the original, handwritten manuscript in which Carroll wrote the tale for the Misses Liddell, he himself provided the pictures, which are somewhat primitive but quite amiable and served as sketches for Tenniel to work with. But in "the after-time," this lack of narrative depiction has added richness to the license of subsequent illustrators to depict Alice herself, and the eccentric individuals she meets, not to mention the background, settings, and overall style, and to explore their own visions of the text.

Tenniel himself occasionally was at variance with the manuscript: for instance, Alice's revelation in Chapter Two—"'I'm sure I'm not Ada,' she said, 'for her hair goes in such long ringlets, and mine doesn't go in ringlets at all'"—is contradicted in Tenniel's pictures. We do know that her hair was long and possibly

untidy, however, thanks to the Hatter's remark, "Her hair wants cutting." There was no particular child model for Tenniel's Alice. As Carroll said in a letter (March 31, 1892) to fellow illustrator E. Gertrude Thomson, "Mr. Tenniel is the only artist, who has drawn for me, who resolutely refused to use a model, and declared he no more needed one than I should need a multiplication-table to work a mathematical problem!" A ridiculous canard involving a photograph of one Mary Hilton Badcock keeps making the rounds, but has been thoroughly discredited (Tenniel's Alice was fully formed and in Carroll's hands six months before he even saw Mary's picture).

The second reason for the work's appeal to such a wide variety of artists is how radical a literary departure it was, how deeply it dives into the unconscious, and how accurately it portrays the topsy-turvy, ironic, paradoxical, incomprehensible, unexpected, and truly funny world in which we live. It simply encouraged a different type of imagination than had ever appeared before, stretching the movement and range of illustrative art.

The two books constitute an artifact of the shared mind, perhaps the first secular infusion into the world of literature of a certain type: the literature of the "collective unconscious," to use Carl Jung's phrase. Freud's discovery of the extent to which our "conscious" life is controlled by the unconscious hints at the ineluctable importance of the role of language in this process. We enter, by rabbit hole or looking-glass, into the realm of magic—metaphor, inspiration, genius, imagination, humor. The tradition was brought to the daylight world for the first time by Lewis Carroll, who invoked, by innovative linguistics, this dark realm of Chaos and Old Night, and of splendors undreamed, in an attempt to portray the dream state by the drifting and merging of identities and personalities, and the multilayered use of language to reach the unconscious: not only to describe it, but to actively stimulate its use.

In a letter to Tom Taylor (later the editor of *Punch*) dated June 10, 1864, Carroll discussed what title to give the work, saying "Of these [titles] I at present prefer 'Alice's Adventures in Wonderland.' In spite of your 'morality,' I want something sensational." The word is appropriate. As Professor James Kincaid stated in his introduction to the Pennyroyal *Alice*, "In any event, the work clearly takes sensational risks, issuing attacks and invitations in all directions. . . . How is it that this apparently innocent children's story is so hospitable, seeming to welcome a nearly unlimited number of approaches and explanations? . . . Carroll applies continuous pressure to the forms and models we use to think about such things as space, time, logic, language, meaning, authority, and death."

It is rare to read these days an "artist's state-ment" by an illustrator of Carroll's works that does not in some way allude to his or her childhood memories of the books. Even the "Golden Age" illustrators featured in this vol-ume were old enough to have read *Alice* when they were young.

One reason that Alice herself has been depicted over the decades in such different ways is that she presents an identity in constant flux. In Wonderland, she doesn't know who she is, has no cultural conventions to fall back upon, and is experiencing an altogether subjec-tive reality, morphing in size and avoiding a fixed essence. As Adriana Peliano, founder of the Lewis Carroll Society of Brazil, has put it, Alice "has become a mirror to collective trans-formations. We re-create images of ourselves. In the present day, even the concept of identity has changed; to ask 'Who are you?' has a dif-ferent meaning. We now know that identity is always changing, and can be multiplied within a single being. Alice's mirror has become a kaleidoscope."

In a six-part series of articles in the *Knight Letter,* the journal of the Lewis Carroll Society of North America (Nos. 76–80), "Evolution of a Dream-Child: Images of Alice and Chang-ing Conceptions of Childhood," Victoria Sears Goldman discussed this topic as well:

What is it about Carroll's vision that has such allure? Perhaps it has some-thing to do with our culture's practice of defining itself by redefining itself over time based on cultural icons—includ-ing fictional characters such as Alice. After the publication of Carroll's book, Alice immediately became the iconic child. There is something about the emblematic figure of Alice and her as-sociations to which we are continuously attracted. Just as childhood is central to Western culture, so Alice is to child-hood. Why has Alice become especially privileged and powerful among fictional characters? I suggest that the charac-ter of Alice is re-imagined generation

after generation so as to ensure that our culture always has a fictional character around which to define itself; a child through whom we can live vicariously, into whom we can channel our fears, dreams, and desires.

Each significant era in the history of childhood has produced its own new version of Alice, and as each is rendered obsolete, the subsequent generation of artists is challenged to replace her with one that is more relevant. . . . Is "child-hood" a universal, timeless phase of life that is characterized by certain constant truths? Or is it a highly malleable social construct? To what extent are artistic representations of children shaped by contemporaneous conceptions of child-hood?

Lastly, *Alice*'s pervasiveness in our culture today is unarguable; it is the most widely quoted novel ever written, whose characters and catchphrases find a way into our every-day lives via political cartoons and speeches, amusement park rides, toys, movies, parapher-nalia, websites, and much more. Dozens of editions of the books appear every year, not to mention biographies, bibliographies, academic treatises, collections of essays, satires and pastiches, and the like. There are very active Lewis Carroll Societies in North America, the United Kingdom, Japan, and Brazil. The search term "Wonderland" may get 44 million or more "hits" on Google. Tim Burton's noisome film, emphatically not a version of *Alice in Wonderland* but bearing its title, grossed a billion dollars worldwide, near the top of the all-time list. The works have been translated into (depending on definition) at least a hundred languages. A copy of the 1865 edition of *Wonderland* sold in 1998 for more than $1.5 million. Alice is as recognizable an icon in this global culture as Mickey Mouse or Snoopy.

The text has been in the public domain for over a century, and a market is more or less guaranteed. What publisher would not want to enter into the fray, with an unheralded—or greatly heralded—new illustrator? Or offer something elegant, or affordable, or what-have-you, retaining Tenniel's work?

As Alice said at the Tea Party, "There's plenty of room!"

MARK BURSTEIN
President
The Lewis Carroll Society of North America

Alice in Wonderland

JESSIE WILLCOX SMITH, 1923

A Knave painting the roses red

Harry Rountree, 1908

Notes on the Illustrations

Lewis Carroll's *Alice's Adventures in Wonderland* is a landmark piece of writing on many fronts. Written nearly one hundred and fifty years ago, this story created to entertain children has never lost its appeal—but the interest adults have in reading the story to children and in exploring it themselves is something special. Most children's stories tend to simplify and brighten reality, while *Alice*, from the start, was complex, unpredictable, and somewhat twisted. Against all conventions, it succeeded in finding an audience and maintaining it, as very few tales do.

A key to the attraction of Wonderland is the wildly imaginative creatures that populate it. With the connections that all of these creatures have to our everyday world, whether it be ordinary field animals or playing cards, they have all been transformed in Carroll's tales to become something they are not. This encourages the imagination, both in the reader, and in the artist. It pushes an illustrator to go even further with the task at hand—to provide the visual clues that define the identity of a character. Carroll has given creative minds a running jump to approach this task, and the long list of the tale's illustrators have embraced it.

Alice's Adventures in Wonderland and *Through the Looking Glass* have become two of the most-often illustrated books in the history of children's publishing. The list of their illuminated editions is incomparable. While it is not our intention to share the breadth of that selection in this volume, it is our hope to represent some of the best, most imaginative, and innovative depictions of the world in which Lewis Carroll placed Alice. For those reasons and others, there are works by some of the most storied artists of the last two centuries. Sir John Tenniel was Alice's first published illustrator. He set a high bar in imagination for all the artists who would follow, not only in Alice's original adventures, but in *Through the Looking Glass and What Alice Saw There* as well. The Jabberwock he designed for that volume was intended to be the frontispiece, but in an informal poll that Carroll took, it was advised that it was too frightening an image to lead off the book . . . Carroll went with the safer option. Today Tenniel's Jabberwock remains one of his best-known images.

Golden Age illustration stars such as Arthur Rackham and Charles Robinson rose to the occasion in 1907 when *Alice's Adventures in Wonderland* entered the public domain.

In a scramble to provide a new look to the beloved story, as many as eight illustrated editions of *Alice's Adventures in Wonderland* came out in that year alone. Two other contributors to the 1907 editions— W. H. Walker and Millicent Sowerby— are found within. Following that group, there would be a flurry of further activity for a decade and a little more, on both sides of the Atlantic.

Years later, in 1929, Willy Pogány gave Alice a contemporary look, with a bobbed haircut and a plaid skirt—at home in the 1920s. The look was anything but traditional, finding its place with those who loved the novelty of the tale but saw the mid-nineteenth-century styles as outdated rather than classic.

In more recent memory, a premier American artist met the challenge of *Alice* with a traditionally classic approach. Barry Moser's woodcuts for the Pennyroyal Press editions nearly bring us full circle in technique—but the work harbors a style and creates a mood that Sir John Tenniel could only dream of.

The images of Wonderland, and the artist's task of capturing them, seem to show no end of attraction to new attempts. No doubt the era of digital illustration will invite new efforts to depict Alice's topsy-turvy world.

Jeff A. Menges
August 2011

The Plates

Sir John Tenniel (1820-1914)
1865 and 1872

Sir John Tenniel's importance to the visuals of Wonderland cannot be overstated. As the story's original illustrator in 1865, Tenniel created 42 line pieces that depicted all of the significant characters. The book's huge success made Tenniel's illustrations definitive for *Alice*, and it is likely that Tenniel's edition has been available in reprint form continuously since its original publication. When Carroll's "revisit" to Wonderland in *Through the Looking Glass and What Alice Found There* came up in 1872, Tenniel initially turned down Carroll's offer to illustrate it. While both author and illustrator had benefited greatly from the success of Wonderland, they had many disagreements on its depiction, which caused Tenniel to pass up the offer. Only after Carroll's unsuccessful attempts to attract another illustrator (possibly due to his reputation for being difficult, or the looming task of following the iconic Tenniel drawings) did Tenniel agree.

Originally better known for magazine illustration—Tenniel was for some time a staff illustrator for *Punch*—he produced or contributed to several illustrated books before his fame with *Alice's Adventures in Wonderland*, including *Undine* and *Aesop's Fables*.

The White Rabbit, and Alice

SIR JOHN TENNIEL

The King and Queen of Hearts were seated on their throne

Sir John Tenniel

a. "Curiouser and curiouser!" b. Scurried away into the darkness as hard as he could go
c. "Twinkle, twinkle, little bat! How I wonder what you're at!"
d. "Hand it over here," said the Dodo

SIR JOHN TENNIEL

a. Advice from a caterpillar   b. "There goes Bill!"
c. And yet you incessantly stand on your head—

SIR JOHN TENNIEL

The Jabberwock

Sir John Tenniel

Peter Newell (1862–1924)
1901

More than one American publisher produced an edition while the British copyright was still in place. The Harper and Brothers edition with illustrations by Peter Newell was published in 1901, followed by sister volumes of *Through the Looking Glass* and *The Hunting of the Snark*. While Newell produced an elaborate and fresh edition, with halftone images and intricate repeating decorations, its reception was mixed, largely due to the complete dominance that the Tenniel drawings had stamped on the story.

Whereas Tenniel's background had largely been political satire and caricature, Newell was more of a pure cartoonist, telling a visual story for the humor it might provide. He created many children's books that used visual devices to further their uniqueness and is seen as a pioneer in children's humor publishing.

"Now I'm opening out like the largest telescope that ever was!"

On various pretexts they all moved off

PETER NEWELL

The Caterpillar and Alice looked at each other

PETER NEWELL

Then they both bowed low and their curls got entangled

PETER NEWELL

They lived at the bottom of a well

Peter Newell

Arthur Rackham (1867–1939)
1907

After Tenniel created the visuals to populate Wonderland, there is little doubt that any edition was more eagerly anticipated than Arthur Rackham's 1907 edition—while many felt that the reimagining of Wonderland by any illustrator was unnecessary, Rackham was already a star in the children's book market, and high expectations for this edition were placed on his shoulders. He delivered a more mature Alice for London publisher William Heinemann, as well as some of the first images of Alice to be printed in full-color. His edition was better received than the others that came out that same year, and time has proven it to be one of the best-loved adaptations.

Arthur Rackham could be considered the leading figure in all of children's book illustration for the first half of the twentieth century. He had a long and prolific career, producing memorable and highly sought-after editions, from fairy tales to Shakespeare.

The Pool of Tears

They all crowded round it panting and asking, "But who has won?"

ARTHUR RACKHAM

"Why, Mary Ann, what are you doing out here?"

Arthur Rackham

ALICE'S·ADVENTURES
IN·WONDERLAND
BY·LEWIS·CARROLL
ILLUSTRATED·BY
ARTHUR·RACKHAM

WITH A PROEM BY AUSTIN DOBSON

LONDON·WILLIAM·HEINEMANN
NEW·YORK·DOUBLEDAY·PAGE·&·C°

Title page design

ARTHUR RACKHAM

The Gryphon

ARTHUR RACKHAM

An unusually large saucepan flew close by it, and very nearly carried it off

ARTHUR RACKHAM

A Mad Tea Party

ARTHUR RACKHAM

The Mock Turtle drew a long breath and said, "That's very curious"

ARTHUR RACKHAM

At this the whole pack rose up into the air, and came flying down upon her

ARTHUR RACKHAM

Charles Robinson (1870–1937)
1907

Not to stand by idly while the Heinemann edition was produced, many other publishers in England took the opportunity to produce a premier edition of *Alice* as its original copyright expired. The scramble came for a top-tier illustrator who could deliver something different from the expectations of the Rackham edition and the original Tenniel drawings. Charles Robinson was an excellent pick for Cassell and Company. Though his color plates may not have drawn the appeal of Rackham's, his distinct line, with its heavy use of solid blacks, grants this edition a captivating graphic quality, separating it immediately from those that depict Alice for a more juvenile market. Robinson imagined a slightly darker side to Wonderland, and may have opened the door to more of that interpretation that would follow in later years.

One of three brothers who held successful careers in the illustration market, Charles was the first to do an edition of *Alice*. Charles Robinson had a strong career in classic children's stories, with book illustration being the focus of his productivity. His older brother, Thomas Heath Robinson, tried his hand at the tale in 1922.

Untitled illustration of the Royal Court

She took down a jar from one of the shelves as she passed

CHARLES ROBINSON

There was a large pool all around her about four inches deep
and reaching half down the hall

CHARLES ROBINSON

a. Advice from a caterpillar b. It was the White Rabbit returning,
splendidly dressed c. "I beg your pardon," said Alice very humbly

CHARLES ROBINSON

"What day of the month is it?" he said, turning to Alice

CHARLES ROBINSON

And in she went

CHARLES ROBINSON

The whole pack rose up into the air

CHARLES ROBINSON

Millicent Sowerby (1878–1967)
1907

One of the few tales of the period with a strong female lead, adventurous and inquisitive, *Alice's Adventures in Wonderland* has always attracted women illustrators. Millicent Sowerby was one of the earliest to illustrate *Alice,* as part of the 1907 group. Sowerby had established herself as an illustrator of girls' subjects, and would have been considered a "natural" for a publisher to select for work on *Alice.* It was not the only pairing she would have with a big name in the children's market—she produced a number of works with Robert Louis Stevenson, in addition to a long-running group of works she did with her sister, Githa.

The Rabbit ... scurried away into the darkness as hard as he could go

There was a table set out under a tree and the March Hare and the Hatter . . .
were having tea at it

MILLICENT SOWERBY

In despair she put her hand in her pocket

MILLICENT SOWERBY

She uncorked it and put it to her lips

Millicent Sowerby

The Queen of Hearts, she made some tarts, All on a summer day

MILLICENT SOWERBY

W. H. Walker (active 1905–1915?)
1907

Whereas W. H. Walker can be connected to few children's books of the period, the contribution he made to the Alice canon has had lasting merit. The brightly colored palette of his Alice illustrations make them quite distinct, without burying the draftsmanship of his line drawings.

The players all played at once, without waiting their turns

W. H. Walker

The cook threw a frying-pan after her as she went out, but it just missed her

W. H. Walker

"I want a clean cup," interrupted the hatter; "Let's all move one place on"

W. H. WALKER

a. Alice was a little startled by seeing the Cheshire Cat sitting on a bough of a tree
b. The White Rabbit read out at the top of his shrill little voice
c. The Queen was in a furious passion, shouting, "Off with his head!"

W. H. WALKER

Alice began telling them her adventures

W. H. Walker

Harry Rountree (1878–1950)
1908

When looking for editions that stand out from the rest, there is no discounting the 1908 *Alice* illustrated by Harry Rountree. Not only are all of the illustrations in full-color—a quite rare and expensive endeavor at the time—but there are 92 of them, from vignetted details to full pages. Rountree's brush has a freshness to it, painting with a more traditional usage of watercolor and encouraging the white highlights of the paper to shine through (uncommon for children's book illustration in 1908). Aside from this unusual application of the medium, Rountree had another facet that made Alice a great choice for him. In earlier works he had displayed a fantastic ability to characterize animals; it had become a specialty of sorts, which he was able to take full advantage of in the characters of Wonderland.

"A cat may look at a king"

HARRY ROUNTREE

a. She knelt down and looked along the passage
b. The rabbit started violently
c. Birds of a feather

HARRY ROUNTREE

44

The mouse gave a sudden leap

HARRY ROUNTREE

a.

b.

a. A Caucus-Race and a Long Tale
b. "Come away, my dears"

HARRY ROUNTREE

46

They all moved off

HARRY ROUNTREE

The frying-pan just missed her

HARRY ROUNTREE

"You're thinking about something, my dear"

Harry Rountree

They began solemnly dancing round and round Alice

HARRY ROUNTREE

All persons more than a mile high to leave the court

HARRY ROUNTREE

Mabel Lucie Attwell (1879–1964)
1910

Few illustrators have approached the task of *Alice* with more personal flair than Mabel Lucie Attwell. Attwell had already illustrated several books and done a good deal of magazine work when she tackled *Alice in Wonderland* for Raphael Tuck in 1910. Her style was readily identifiable—with a friendly, simple manner—she was a pioneer in the direction of children's book illustration that would carry on through the twentieth century. The strength she had in the characterization of children made her a popular choice for children's stories. Add to this the limited palette of color that she worked with in her *Alice* pieces, and hers are some of the most unique in all the color-plate editions of the period.

"Oh dear! Oh dear! I shall be too late!"

MABEL LUCIE ATTWELL

The White Rabbit's House

MABEL LUCIE ATTWELL

The Pig Baby

MABEL LUCIE ATTWELL

a. The Fish-Footman began by producing from under his arm a great letter
b. Then followed the Knave of Hearts, carrying the King's crown
on a crimson velvet cushion

Mabel Lucie Attwell

The Mad Hatter's Tea-party

MABEL LUCIE ATTWELL

The Mock Turtle's Story

Mabel Lucie Attwell

The trial of the Knave of Hearts

MABEL LUCIE ATTWELL

George Soper (1870–1942)
1910

Before the book boom of the early twentieth century, George Soper had done well establishing himself in English periodicals that carried a great deal of line illustration. His success with children's magazines like *The Captain* led to the opportunity to illustrate books in color. Soper landed assignments for many of the classic titles that were being republished at the time—Lamb's *Tales from Shakespeare* in 1909 preceded his edition of *Alice in Wonderland*, and later he would add titles such as *The Arabian Nights*, *The Water-Babies*, and *Tanglewood Tales* to his resume. His passion for line art returned to him in the 1920s, when he pursued etching in addition to maintaining a career in illustration. Soper's two daughters also carved out careers in art; his second daughter, Eileen, became a successful illustrator in her own right.

The cat vanished quite slowly, beginning with
the end of the tail and ending with the grin

GEORGE SOPER

" Mine is a long and sad tale," said the mouse

GEORGE SOPER

The executioner had never had to do such a thing before,
and he wasn't going to begin at his time of life

GEORGE SOPER

She came upon a neat little house

GEORGE SOPER

The whole pack rose up into the air, and came flying down upon her

GEORGE SOPER

A. E. Jackson (1873–1952)
1914

A. E. Jackson's illustrations for *Alice* in 1914 show a deep commitment to the work—the careful study of architecture used in the piece that serves as a frontispiece for this volume provides a clue that Jackson really devoted himself to the material. His work also features full and complex compositions and a carefully restricted use of color.

Jackson worked in the illustration field from 1893 to 1947, accomplishing a long list of classic illustrated titles, including *Gulliver's Travels*, *The Water-Babies*, and *Tales from the Arabian Nights*, in addition to regularly working with a number of children's annuals.

LONDON: HENRY·FROWDE: HODDER & STOUGHTON

Title page art

A. E. JACKSON

"No more, thank ye; I'm better now"

A. E. JACKSON

"Please would you tell me," said Alice, a little timidly,
"why your cat grins like that?"

A. E. JACKSON

"Very uncomfortable for the dormouse," thought Alice

A. E. JACKSON

She was exactly the right height to rest her chin on Alice's shoulder

A. E. JACKSON

She tipped over the jury box, upsetting all the jurymen
on to the heads of the crowd below

A. E. Jackson

The whole pack rose up into the air, and came flying down upon her

A. E. JACKSON

Margaret Tarrant (1888-1959)
1916

The simple and effective use of the vignette helped Margaret Tarrant's edition gain an identity of its own. Already an established book illustrator by the time she took on *Alice's Adventures in Wonderland* for Ward, Lock, in 1916, Tarrant had done a good deal of work for greeting card publishers and had over a dozen book titles to her credit, starting with her edition of *The Water-Babies* in 1908. Though Tarrant often did fairy tale illustration during her career, the latter stage of her professional days were largely occupied with religious works; she traveled to Palestine in 1936 to collect material for those subjects.

"Never!" said the Queen furiously, throwing the inkstand at the Lizard as she spoke

MARGARET TARRANT

The whole pack rose up into the air and came flying down upon her

Margaret Tarrant

They were indeed a queer looking party that assembled on the bank—the birds
with draggled feathers, the animals with their fur clinging close to them,
and all dripping wet, cross and uncomfortable

MARGARET TARRANT

Alice succeeded in getting her flamingo's body tucked away, comfortably
enough, under her arm, but generally, just as she had got its neck nicely
straightened out, it would twist itself round and look up into her face

MARGARET TARRANT

"Then you know," the Mock Turtle went on, "you throw the——"
"The lobsters!" shouted the Gryphon, with a bound into the air.
"—as far out to sea as you can—"

MARGARET TARRANT

Milo Winter (1888–1956)
1916

Milo Winter had found a niche in American publishing, and it was located in Chicago. While most children's book publishing in the first quarter of the twentieth century was coming out of England or the northeast parts of the United States, Winter had partnered with American publisher Rand McNally to become middle America's children's book illustrator. McNally published many of the same classics that came out of London, New York, and Boston, but, with less shipping expense, they had found a market of their own in America's heartland.

Winter's book illustration career really started around 1912, with the publication of a book of Winter's own writing, *Billy Popgun*. Shortly afterwards he began his work with McNally, with whom he would work steadily for the next three decades, producing competitive plate books of classics, of which *Alice* was a welcome addition.

Alice sat down in a large arm-chair at one end of the table

MILO WINTER

"So Bill's got to come down the chimney, has he?"

MILO WINTER

"It is a very good height indeed!" said the caterpillar angrily

MILO WINTER

"It may kiss my hand, if it likes," said the King

MILO WINTER

Alice had seated herself on the bank of a little brook,
and was sawing away with the knife

MILO WINTER

Charles Folkard (1878-1963)
1921

Charles Folkard entered the profession of illustration after designing some of his own flyers to promote his magic act. His continued successes in illustration were almost as diverse—after a short period in magazine work, Folkard got a break in 1910 with his first "gift book," *The Swiss Family Robinson*. The following year, Folkard found a home with a new publisher, A. & C. Black, with whom he would work for the next twenty-seven years. In addition to his book work, Folkard developed a highly successful cartoon strip in 1915 for the *Daily Mail*, called "Teddy Tail."

Folkard's *Alice* imagery first appeared in 1921 in *Songs from Alice in Wonderland and Through the Looking-Glass*, later reprinted in a more traditional edition of the story in 1929.

Alice and her Friends

CHARLES FOLKARD

The Mad Tea-party

CHARLES FOLKARD

The Lobster Quadrille

CHARLES FOLKARD

Yet you balance an eel on the end of your nose

CHARLES FOLKARD

Beautiful Soup

CHARLES FOLKARD

Gwynedd Hudson (active 1910–1935)
1922

There are few shorter, potentially bright careers in book illustration that I have come across in years of research than that of Gwynedd Hudson. Her output in published book work may consist of as few as three books. The third, published in 1922, was her edition of *Alice's Adventures in Wonderland*, which is a fine example of color-plate book work. Twelve plates—beautiful, fully realized paintings—include the cover image of this collection. Hudson's choice to portray the mad hatter's tea-party in an autumn setting distinguishes it from others, providing a color scheme that previous illustrators had not thought to explore, resulting in a freshness without any disrespect for the material. The artist later went on to do more design-related materials, including posters for the London Underground.

Frontispiece, Alice and Dinah

GWYNEDD HUDSON

The poor little Lizard, Bill, was in the middle of being held up by two
Guinea Pigs, who were giving it something out of a bottle

GWYNEDD HUDSON

Advice from a Caterpillar

Gwynedd Hudson

The March Hare and the Hatter were having tea

GWYNEDD HUDSON

The King and Queen of Hearts were seated on their throne

Gwynedd Hudson

Willy Pogány (1882–1955)
1929

The decade that followed World War I was a period crying out for change, and it happened culturally in many ways. Through art, music, design, and fashion, separation from the Victorian era had become complete, and many aspects of the past were left behind.

The need for a fresh approach to a then sixty-five-year-old classic children's tale brought E. P. Dutton to find Willy Pogány. Pogány did something throughout his long and prolific career that few other commercial artists can manage—he changed his style to suit the times. This trait meant that Pogány's *Alice* would be familiar to the children of the day, and not look as if it were from an "old-fashioned tale." Pogány did it well, and gave us a distinctive *Alice* that tells us of the time she is from, rather than the period Carroll wrote.

They were indeed a queer-looking party

WILLY POGÁNY

Left Endpaper

WILLY POGÁNY

Right Endpaper

WILLY POGÁNY

A Mad Tea-Party

Willy Pogány

a.

b.

a. The roses growing on it were white, but there were three gardeners at it,
busily painting them red
b. "Oh, I beg your pardon!" she exclaimed in a tone of great dismay

WILLY POGÁNY

Barry Moser (b. 1940)
1983

One of the most interesting editions to be produced in the last half-century is one that returned to the roots of *Alice* images, containing only line art. Barry Moser's moody portraits and outstanding technical skill as a woodcut artist made this unlike any previous edition. Moser has the ability to place great character in his figures, and the plates he produced for his editions of *Alice's Adventures in Wonderland* and *Through the Looking Glass* are no exception. In Moser's art, the characters of *Alice* have become iconic, and they provide a statement in their visual presentation alone.

The Frog

BARRY MOSER

105

106

The White Knight

(facing page) The Red Queen

BARRY MOSER

Tweedle Dum

Barry Moser

and Tweedle Dee

BARRY MOSER

Red Knight

BARRY MOSER

110

THE
END

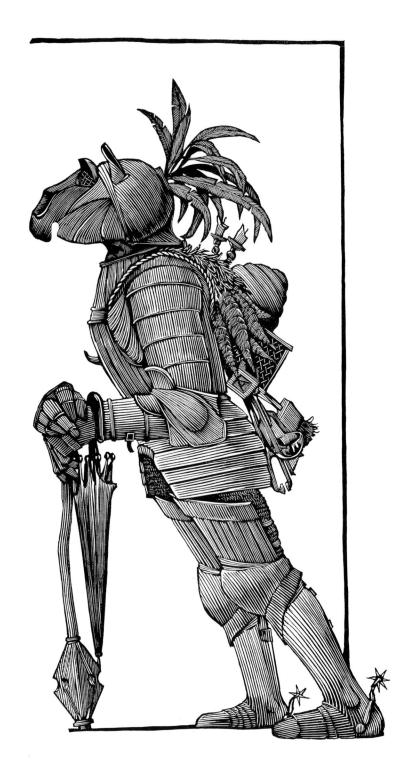

White Knight

BARRY MOSER